ANIMALS
That Make a Difference!

Eagles

Ande Denise Down

Explore other books at:
WWW.ENGAGEBOOKS.COM

VANCOUVER, B.C.

WWW.ENGAGEBOOKS.COM

Eagles: Level 3
Animals That Make a Difference!
Down, Ande Denise, 1990
Text © 2023 Engage Books
Design © 2023 Engage Books

Edited by: A.R. Roumanis,
Sarah Harvey, Melody Sun, and Ashley Lee
Design by: Rose Gowsell Pattison

Text set in Arial Regular.
Chapter headings set in Arial Black.

FIRST EDITION / FIRST PRINTING

LIBRARY AND ARCHIVES CANADA CATALOGUING IN PUBLICATION

Title: Eagles / Ande Denise Down.
Names: Down, Ande Denise, author.
Description: Series statement: Animals that make a difference

Identifiers: Canadiana (print) 2023044864x | Canadiana (ebook) 20230448658
ISBN 978-1-77476-836-5 (hardcover)
ISBN 978-1-77476-837-2 (softcover)
ISBN 978-1-77476-838-9 (EPUB)
ISBN 978-1-77476-839-6 (PDF)
ISBN 978-1-77878-136-0 (audio)

Subjects:
LCSH: Eagles—Juvenile literature.
LCSH: Human-animal relationships—Juvenile literature.

Classification: LCC QL696.F32 D69 2023 | DDC J598.9/42—DC23

This project has been made possible in part by the Government of Canada.

Canada

Contents

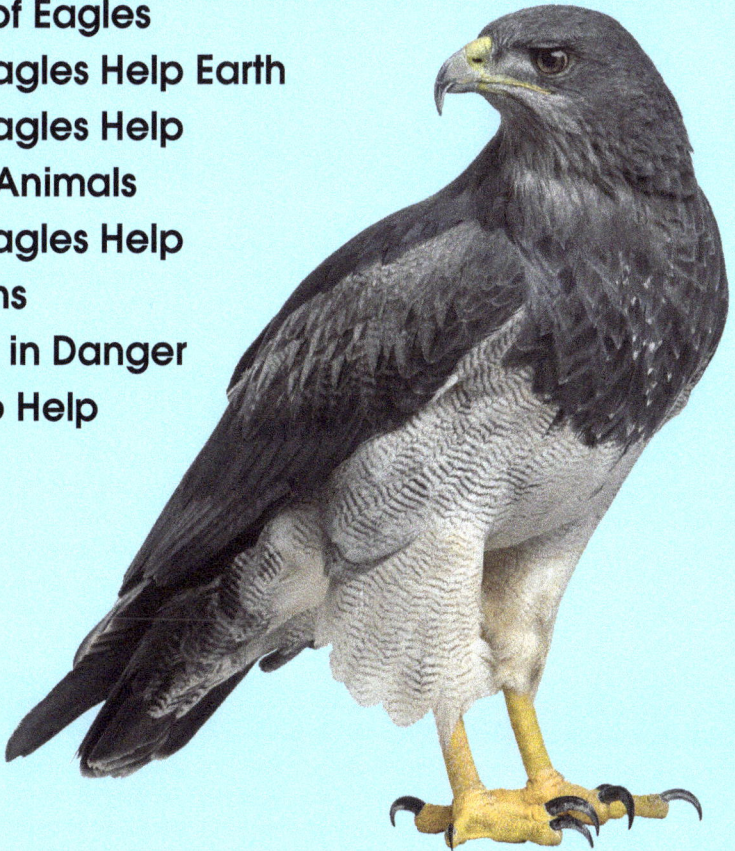

What Are Eagles?

Eagles are a kind of raptor. Raptors are birds that hunt other animals for food. There are over 60 **species** of eagles in the world.

KEY WORD

Species: a group of similar animals or plants that can make babies with each other.

Eagles have larger wings than most birds. Moving their wings up and down takes a lot of energy. Larger wings help them **glide** for longer periods of time. When they glide, they do not need to flap their wings as often.

KEY WORD

Glide: move smoothly and easily.

A Closer Look

Eagles come in many different sizes. The smallest eagles are only about 16 inches (40 centimeters) tall. The largest eagles can be up to 3 feet (1 meter) tall.

Eagles have good eyesight. They can see a rabbit from about 2 miles (3.2 kilometers) away.

Eagles have hooked beaks. They clean their beaks by rubbing them on rocks or trees.

They have four toes on each foot. Each toe has a big claw called a talon.

Where Do Eagles Live?

Eagles live near forests, mountains, deserts, or water. Their nests are at the top of trees. Eagle nests are made of sticks, plants, and feathers.

Bald eagle nests are 5 to 6 feet (1.5 to 1.8 meters) wide.

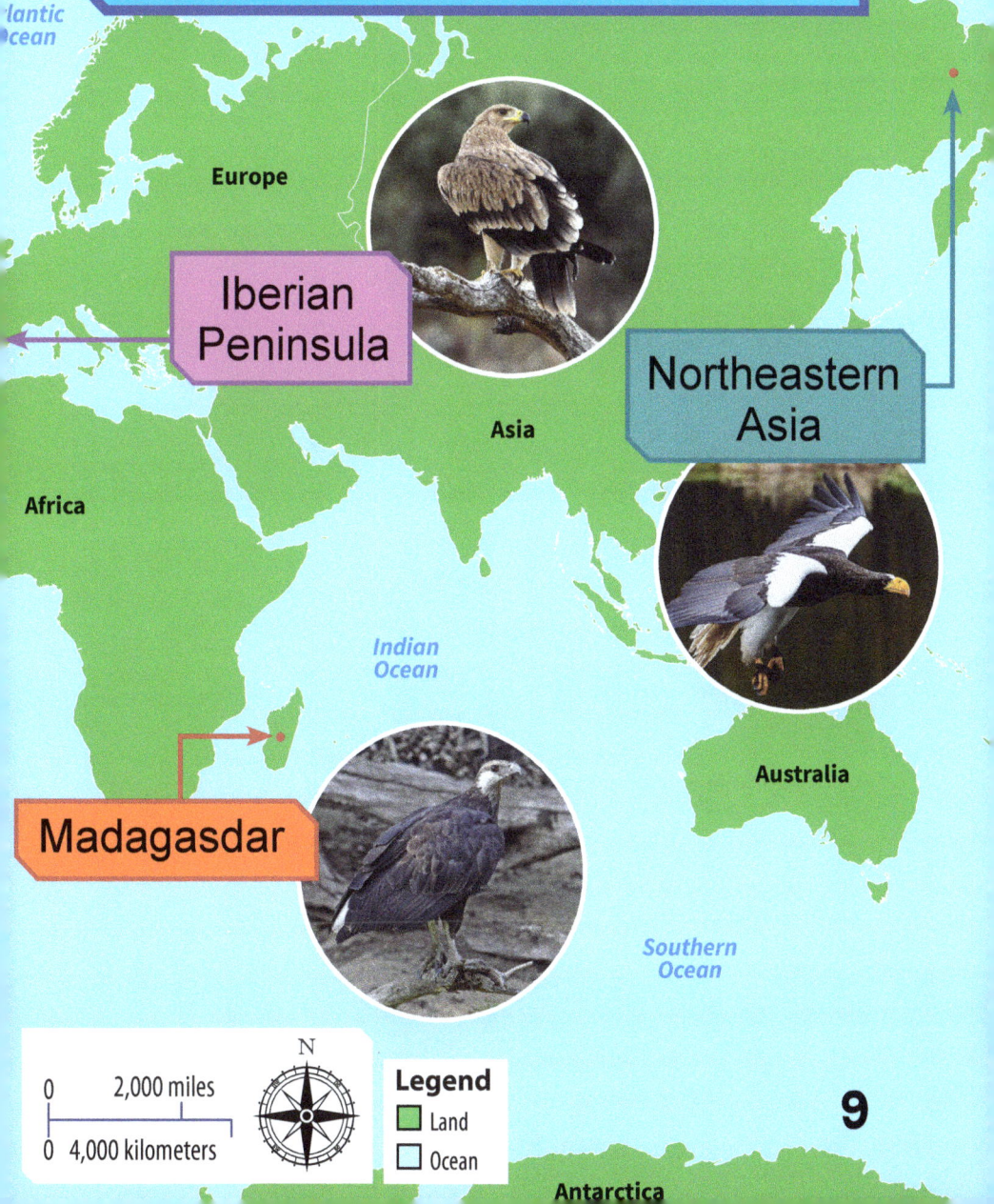

Eagles live everywhere except Antarctica. The Madagascar fish eagle only lives in Madagascar. The Spanish imperial eagle is found on the Iberian Peninsula. Steller's sea eagle lives in northeastern Asia.

Arctic Ocean

Atlantic Ocean

Europe

Iberian Peninsula

Asia

Northeastern Asia

Africa

Indian Ocean

Australia

Madagasdar

Southern Ocean

0   2,000 miles

0   4,000 kilometers

N

Legend
Land
Ocean

9

Antarctica

What Do Eagles Eat?

Eagles are **carnivores**. Young eagles find dead animals to eat. When they grow up, they learn to hunt. Adult eagles hunt animals like fish, birds, and rabbits.

KEY WORD

Carnivores: animals that only eat other animals.

Eagles use their sharp talons to grab animals. They use their hooked beaks to rip the food apart. Adult eagles bring food back to their nests for their babies. They tear it into small pieces for them.

Eagles dive into the water to catch fish.

How Do Eagles Talk to Each Other?

Eagles screech, whistle, cry, and chirp. Their sounds are high-pitched. Baby eagles chirp to call for food. Adult females whistle to get the attention of male eagles.

Male and female eagles will often do a sky dance before they make babies. They join their feet together and then spin downward. At the last second, they let go and fly upward. This helps them form a close relationship.

Eagle Life Cycle

Mother eagles usually lay two eggs. The mother and father take turns sitting on the eggs. Baby eagles called eaglets hatch after about 35 days.

Eagles learn to fly at three months old. Young eagles learn to hunt by watching their parents. Once an eagle can hunt, it leaves to live by itself.

Eagles become adults when they are about five years old. They find another eagle to make babies with. This other eagle is called their mate. Most eagles stay with the same mate for life.

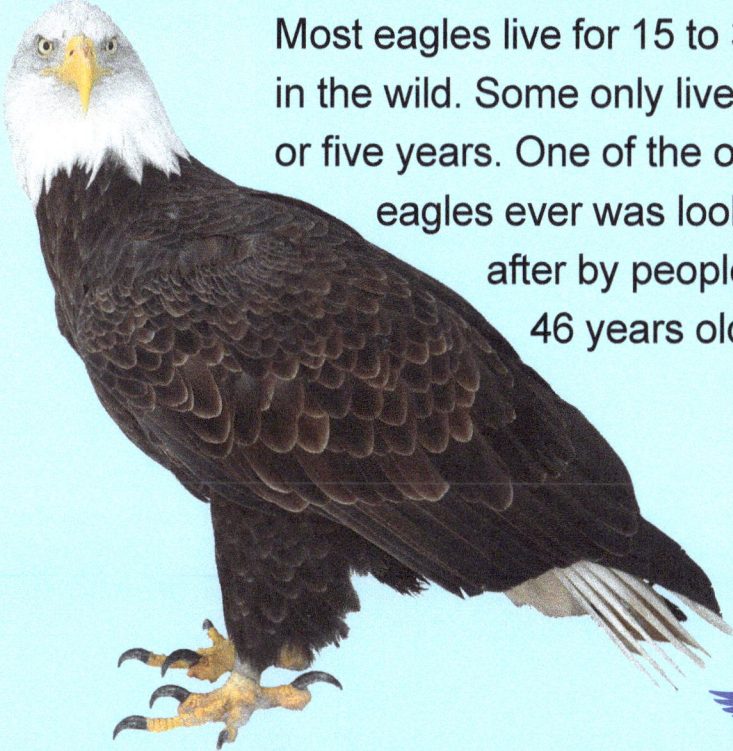

Most eagles live for 15 to 30 years in the wild. Some only live for four or five years. One of the oldest eagles ever was looked after by people. It was 46 years old.

Curious Facts About Eagles

Adult bald eagles can be as long as 8 feet (2.4 meters) from one wing tip to the other.

Eagles are apex predators. This means no other animals hunt them.

Mates build their nests together.

If an eagle catches a fish that is too big to fly with, it will swim to land with the fish in its talons.

The largest eagle nest ever found was more than 8 feet (2.4 meters) wide and almost 18 feet (5.5 meters) tall.

Eagles have a pouch in their throat called a crop that they store food in.

Kinds of Eagles

The different species of eagles are often split into four groups. Sea eagles live near water and mostly eat fish.

Booted eagles have feathers all the way down to their feet. Their feathers can even cover their toes.

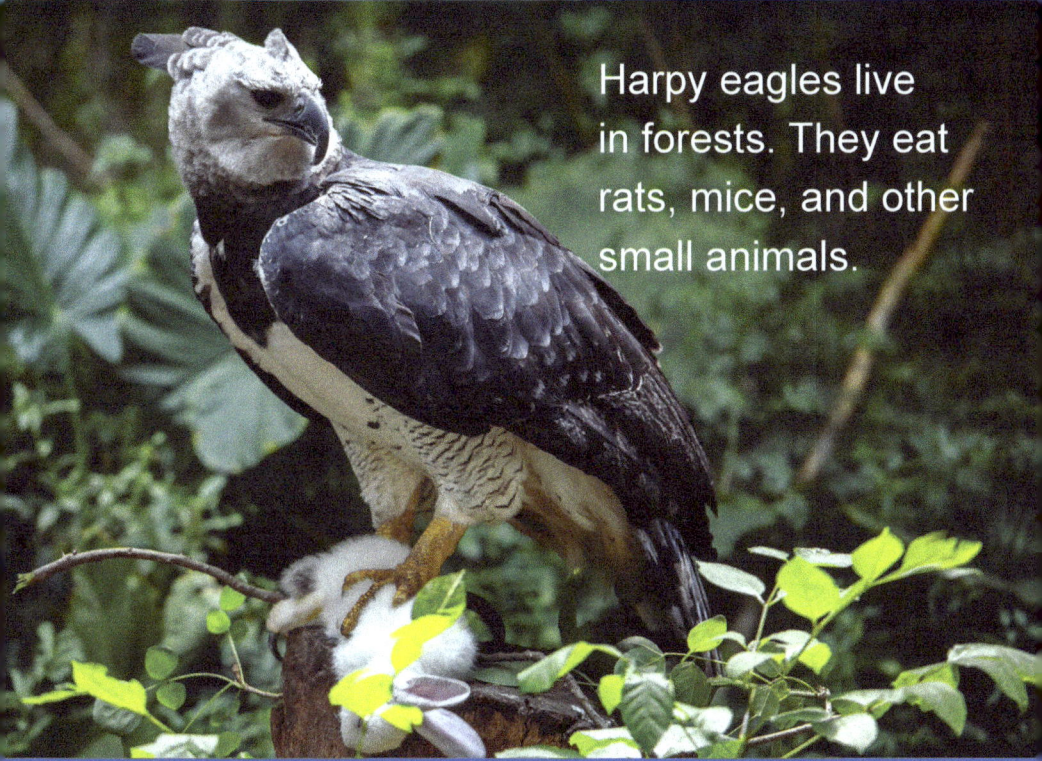

Harpy eagles live in forests. They eat rats, mice, and other small animals.

Snake eagles are mainly found in Africa. They eat snakes. Their toes and legs are covered in scales to protect them from bites.

How Eagles Help Earth

Many animals eat plants. When eagles hunt these animals, it helps make sure there are not too many of them. If there are too many plant-eating animals, plants will not have a chance to grow and spread.

Bald eagles often fight over salmon. The winner of the fight will carry the salmon to a tree. As the winner eats their fish, pieces drop to the ground below. These pieces break down and give the soil **nutrients**. These nutrients are used by plants to grow.

KEY WORD

Nutrients: something in food that help people, animals, and plants live and grow.

How Eagles Help Other Animals

The **bacteria** in dead animals can grow and spread if it is left alone. This bacteria can make other animals sick. When eagles eat dead animals, they stop this bacteria from spreading.

KEY WORD

Bacteria: tiny living things that can cause illness or disease.

Eagles hunt weak and old animals. This helps the strongest and healthiest animals survive. When the strongest animals survive, future **generations** of these animals will become stronger too.

KEY WORD

Generations: a group of living things that are born around the same time.

Eagles have strong stomach acid that kills most of the bacteria they eat.

How Eagles Help Humans

White-tailed eagles went **extinct** in Britain in the early 1900s. They have now returned to the Isle of Mull in Scotland. People from all over the world are traveling there to see them. This is helping local businesses make money.

KEY WORD

Extinct: when an animal population stops existing.

In Mongolia, the Kazakh people train golden eagles to hunt for them. They **rely** on eagles to bring them food. They also use the fur of hunted animals to make clothing.

KEY WORD

Rely: need someone or something for help or support.

Eagles in Danger

Some kinds of eagles are endangered. This means they are at risk of dying out forever. Humans are the biggest danger to eagles. When trees get cut down, eagles lose their **habitat**.

KEY WORD

habitat: the place an animal or plant lives.

Lead is a metal that is sometimes used to make bullets. Eagles often eat small pieces of lead when they eat an animal that has been killed with a lead bullet. This lead is **poisonous** and often makes eagles sick.

Other animals also lose their homes when trees get cut down. This means eagles have less food.

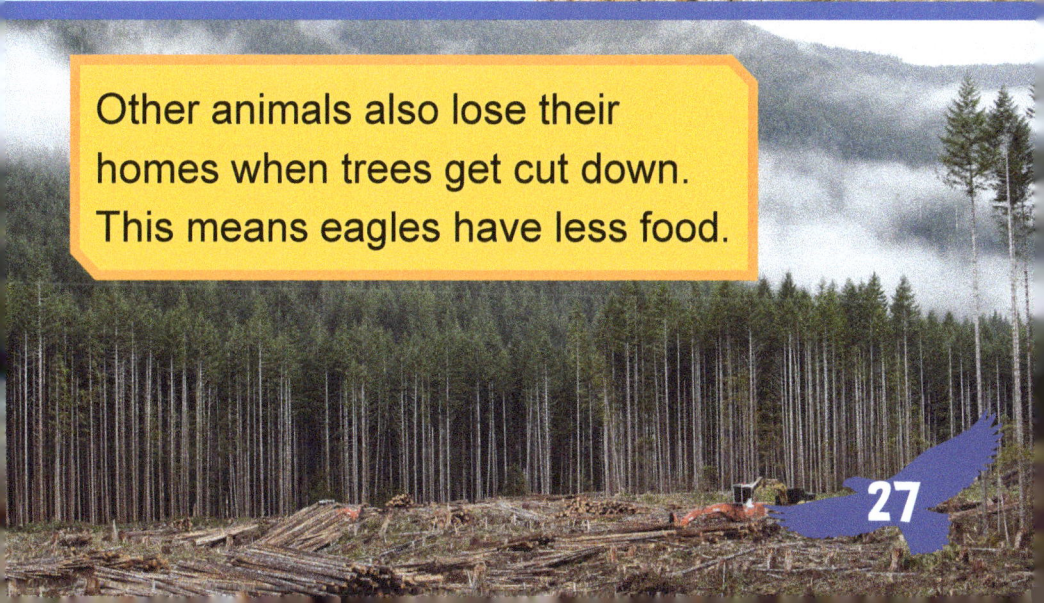

How to Help Eagles

If you see someone bothering an eagle nest, contact your local wildlife center. You should also do this if you see an eagle nest that has fallen out of a tree. They can help keep the eagles and their nests safe.

Stay away from eagle nests. Getting too close can cause eagles to leave and find a new place to make a nest. Young eagles may jump out of the nest before they can fly if they get scared.

Quiz

Test your knowledge of eagles by answering the following questions. The questions are based on what you have read in this book. The answers are listed on the bottom of the next page.

1 How big are the smallest eagles?

2 Where do eagles live?

3 Are eagles carnivores or herbivores?

4 What are baby eagles called?

5 How big was the largest eagle nest ever found?

6 What kind of eagles went extinct in Britain in the early 1900s?

Explore other books in the
Animals That Make a Difference series

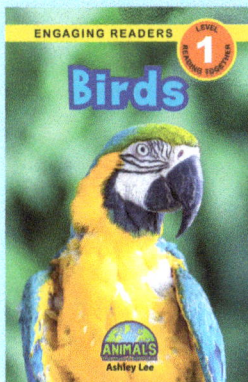

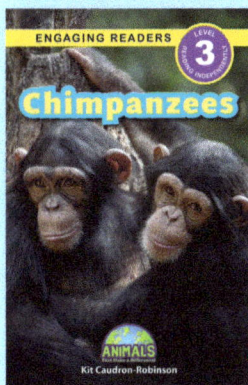

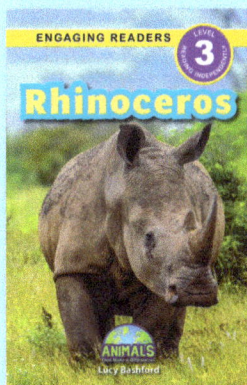

Visit www.engagebooks.com to explore more Engaging Readers.

www.ingramcontent.com/pod-product-compliance
Lightning Source LLC
Chambersburg PA
CBHW052035030426
42337CB00027B/5017